The Northport Arts Coalition presents ...

THE POETRY PATH 2025

The View From Here

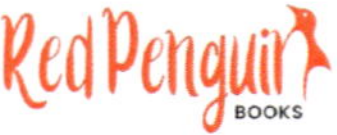

Three years after first floating the idea of a poetry path in our beautiful harborside park past the Village Board, the Northport Arts coalition is thrilled to be inaugurating the second class of poets and artists for the Northport Village Poetry Path. We are so grateful to all the people who have supported and lauded this project.

First and foremost, to Northport Village Deputy Mayor Meghan Dolan who has been behind it 100% from day one. This path would not exist without her collaboration.

To the New York State Council for the Arts and PSEGLI who provided generous grants that kickstarted our fundraising and inspired our sponsors and donors:

James P. Wagner
Linda and David Dickman
Maggie Bloomfield
The Carner Family
Mary Sheila Morrissey
Nolan Funeral Home
Lauren and Daniel Paige
Betty and David Schram
Chip Williford

Finally, to the hundreds of people who have taken a moment out of their busy day to slow down and enjoy the beauty of the path – its words, its art, and its incomparable setting. You are the reason we did this.

Enjoy the Northport Village Poetry Path volume two, "The View From Here."
~ Amy Connor, Executive Director, Northport Arts Coalition

MISSION STATEMENT AND HISTORY

The mission of the Northport Arts Coalition is to inspire and support artists and to promote collaboration and connection within our island community. We embrace all creative disciplines, welcome diversity, and volunteer in the endeavor of planning and sponsoring artistic gatherings. We aspire to bring the arts in all their forms to a varied audience through entertainment, education and participation.

NAC was founded in 1998 by a group of artists dedicated to giving themselves and other artists a way to bring their art to the public. They met once a week at the Northport Historical Society and in private homes. In 1999 NAC was incorporated and received non-profit status. It has since grown into an organization of volunteer arts professionals who work to bring the arts in all their forms to both Northport and the wider community. NAC runs programs in several venues, including NAC Presents! at Northport Library, Friday night Happenings on Main Street free concerts in Northport Park every summer, monthly Poets in Port poetry readings year round, an annual Northport ArtWalk event throughout Northport Village, the annual Art in the Park Festival, and a year-round rotating art exhibit at Daniel Gale's Northport real estate office. In keeping with NAC's mission to bring the arts to the community, all of our events are free to the public so that cost won't be a limitation on who can access the arts.

Board of Directors

Amy Fortgang Connor - Executive Director
Manny Falzon - Music Director
Sandra Ciraolo - Newsletter Coordinator and Webmaster
Linda Trott Dickman - Secretary, Poetry and Spoken Word Director
David L. Dickman - Treasurer

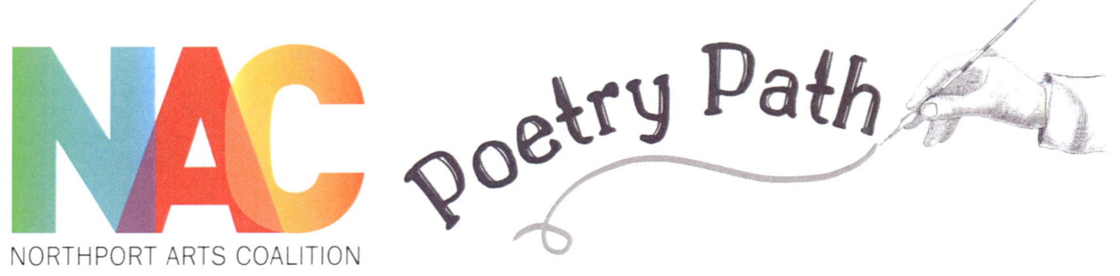

Joyce Kilmer wrote, "I think that I shall never see a poem as lovely as a tree."
The Northport Arts Coalition invites you to enjoy beautiful poetry among the magnificent trees and glorious natural surroundings of the Northport Village Park.

The Northport Arts Coalition thanks the following people and organizations for their support and sponsorship:
Mayor Donna Koch
Village of Northport Board of Trustees
Trustee Meghan Dolan, Commissioner of Parks

Northport Village Poetry Path Exhibit Sponsors:
James P. Wagner
David and Linda Dickman
Maggie Bloomfield
The Carner Family
Mary Sheila Morrissey
Nolan Funeral Home
Lauren and Daniel Paige
Betty and David Schram
Chip Williford

The Northport Village Poetry Path is sponsored in part by generous grants from:
The Huntington Arts Council
New York State Council on the Arts
PSEGLI

FOREWORD

I saw my first Poetry Path in Bellingham, Washington, on a visit. I was immediately drawn in and explored the path and the website where the path's story was told. I contacted the library, the creators of the path, and the contest to see how it was done.
(https://thepoetrydepartment.wordpress.com/2012/08/24/sue-boynton-poetry-walk/)

I walked the path and hoped I could raise excitement for it in the 2012 school year. It was presented to School Principals, Arts Administrators, anyone who would listen, and always, it was a polite response, followed by no action. One fourth-grade student wrote a 'persuasive letter" to convince others that the idea was a good one. She is now in college.

When I mentioned it to Amy Connor, Executive Director of the Northport Arts Coalition, the idea was met with more than a polite response; it was met with immediate support of poetry and a quest for grants and actions to make it happen. As a result of the original idea, shared vision, and the acquisition of the necessary funds and support, the poetry path is happening!

Welcome to this, our second poetry/art collaboration! The poetry came first, and the artists then interpreted the poems. Here are the fruits of our labor, the poems, the art that was paired with them, and the joy of seeing them together in a place where all can enjoy them.

We are in our second year, and just as thrilled. We have garnered attention across the country, across the world. We are so very thankful for our new donors and for this new year on the Poetry Path!

~ Linda Trott Dickman, BSE, MLS, MFA, NYS Woman of Distinction 2023

The Path I Chose
for the Poetry Path 2025

Winds along the water,
 around and under old trees
The frolic of dogs dancing
The music of many
The music of one

The path I chose
stops just before swings,
a merry-go-round, see-saws
amidst happy cries

This path open to many views
An all-weather path
punctuated by poetry

Verses of tar, stanzas of playground
rhythms of swings, seesaws,
Rhymes of rip-rap, ribboned in macadam
the ringing of halyards,
the kisses of the tides,
cushioned in carpets of green

This path I choose,
is for sitting, running, playing
romping, dreaming, drawing, writing,
dedicating, knowing joy and sorrow in concert

Along the harbor it winds
around and under trees
the frolic of dogs dancing
the sound of birds on breeze

The views here are so varied
from boats, to lawn, to swings
so many find an anchor
so much joy it brings

The path I choose, like ribbon
threads all through the park
dotted with thoughtful poems
and art to make it spark

Parades rest, concerts calling
weddings are captured on the pier
prom Kings and Queens and families
observing end of year

This path is so well traveled
enamored by us all
we gather for occasions,
summer spring and fall

No matter what the weather
Or what occasion near
I celebrate this path we walk
and love the view from here.

~ Linda Trott Dickman

Veterans

Poem by JoAnn Proscia
Artwork by Lisa Carrano

Memorial Day 2006, I was revising
a poem to send to David
when I heard the drumbeats
signaling the start of the parade.
I left my unsipped cup of tea,
and headed down the road
in time to see them.
They were followed
by children's baseball teams,
Brownies, volunteer firemen.
People were standing on church steps,
some sat on curbs holding flags,
a few sat on a ledge at the P.O.
their feet atop mailboxes.
Children sat on their father's shoulders.
People were holding babies in their arms,
others dogs on their leashes.
A man dressed in a kilt held up a baby
and kissed her stomach.
She squealed with laughter.
Shopkeepers held sidewalk sales.
I saw wreaths; heard trumpets playing Taps,
prayers and rifle shots.
One was wearing his Army uniform from World War II.
It still fit.
I remembered past parades:
David holding the flag
for the Cub Scouts,
Doug in the Marching Band.
My friend, Mari, saluting the flag.

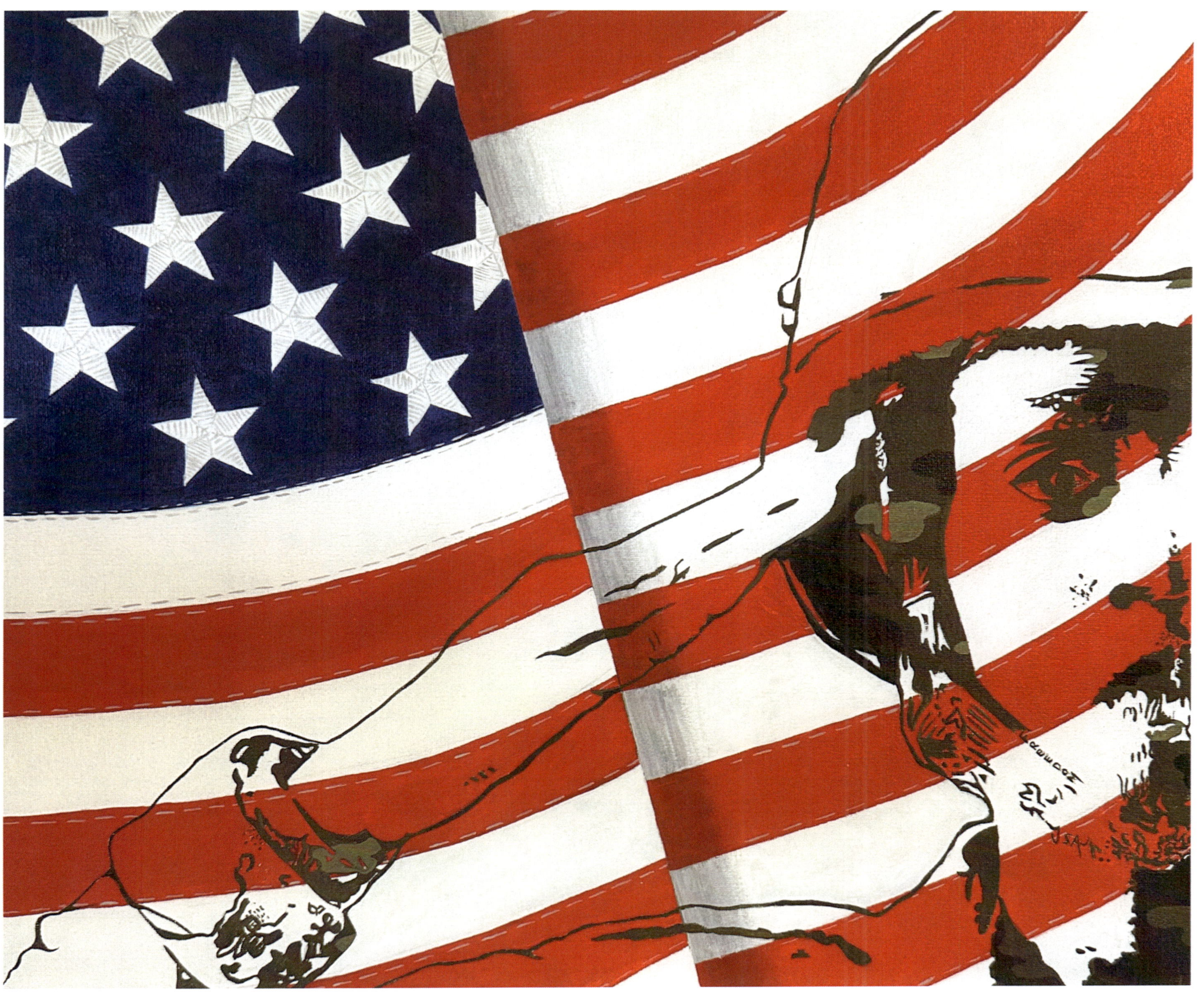

Watershed Moment

Poetry by Emily-Sue Sloane
Artwork by Deidre Elzer-Lento

time melts away
after a hard summer rain

when gray skies make way for blue patches
emerging under the brush of clouds

the smell of the soak rises
droplets glisten on grass

and prism'd puddles
coax steam from pavement

as trees rustle in the breeze
past and present flit by

on the wings of a black butterfly
that doesn't land

though I wait
breath paused

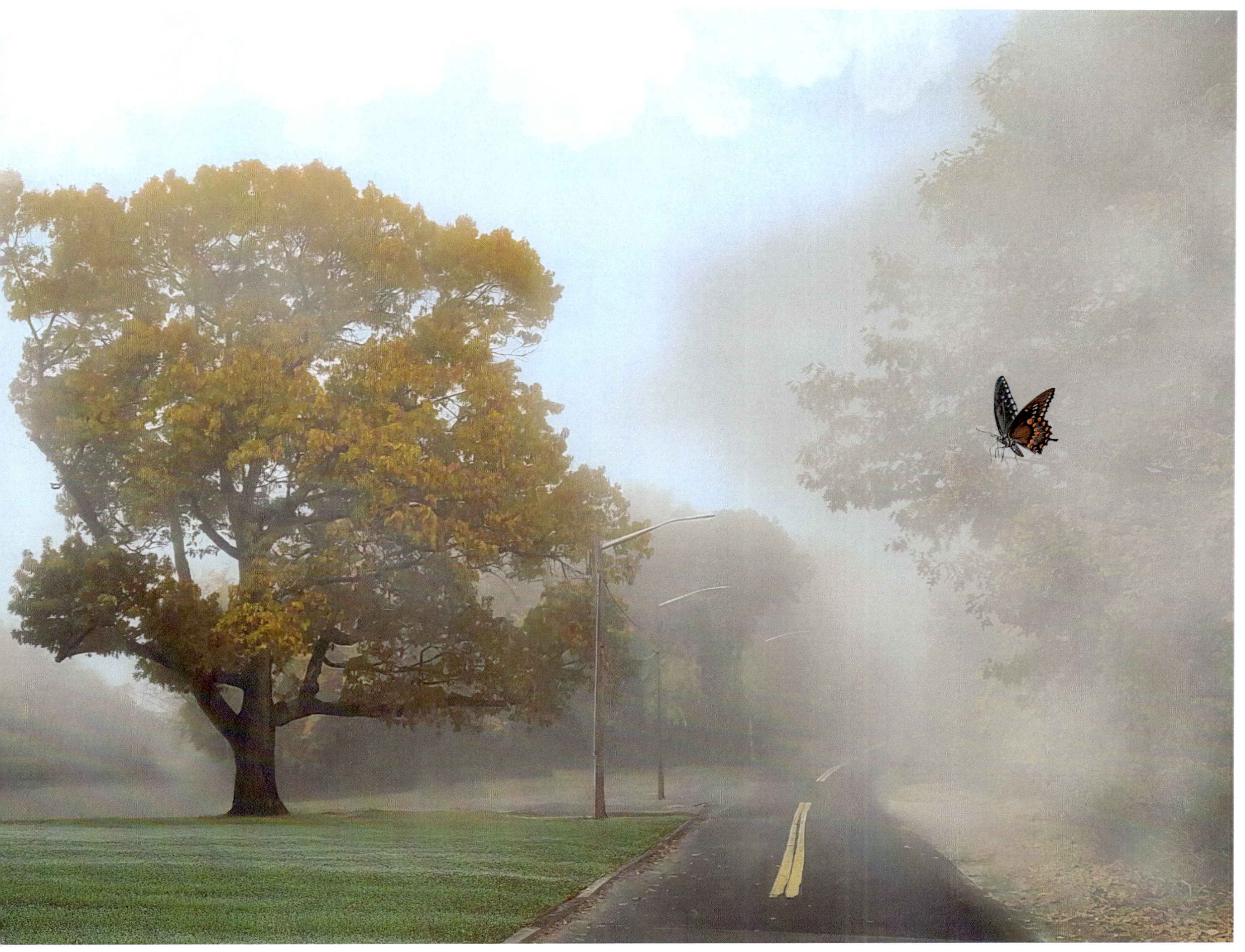

I Sing the Works of Man

Poem by Richard Bronson
Artwork by Loretta Cerame

In twilight, I walked the beach,
watched gulls ride the sea wind.
Light lingered towards a tardy dusk,
sun setting fire to water.

Silent, above the clouds,
made small by stratospheric flight,
a jet traversed the arc of sky,
a bright star in the east,
then gone –

yet its contrail remained, a cursive line
upon amorphous cloud and sky.
What wonder, this Shiva
that has shrunken the Earth,

brought all within day's reach —
brainchild of dreamers
who glimpsed a vision without fear
and grasped it.

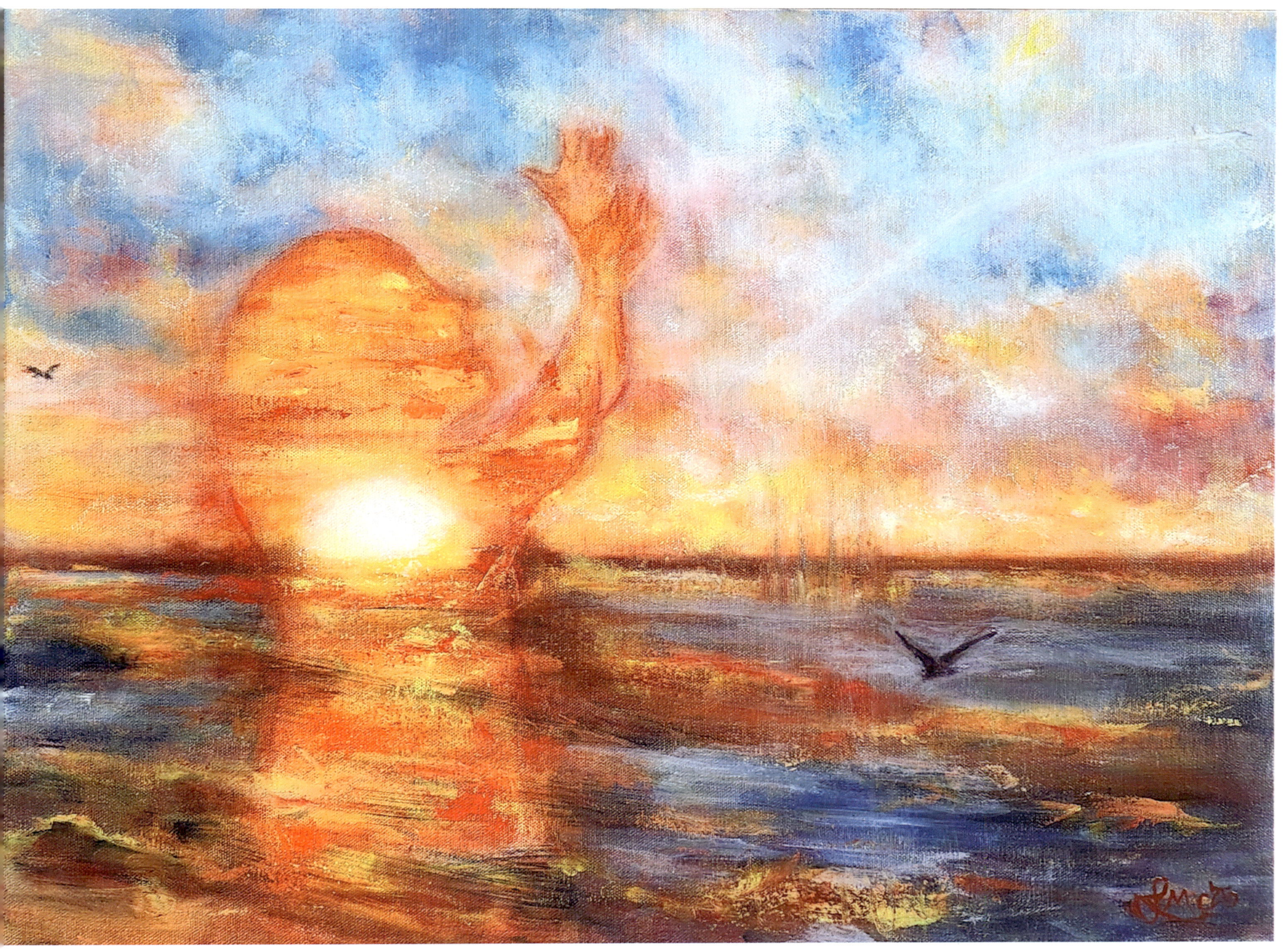

Solidago

Poem by Diana Poulos-Lutz
Artwork by Nancy Panicucci-Roma

I bow down to the seaside goldenrod
with its gleaming yellow, an exquisite

shade of which can hardly be described.
They mostly point upward like hands that aren't

tired but gracefully steadfast. Below my feet
are seldom footprints from recent travelers

no longer here. In this coastal playground for
wandering souls, the goldenrod blooms

strikingly beautiful through late fall, when far
less humans visit here to see their glory.

And for solo travelers in this chilly season
I contemplate--maybe we too can see the reflection

of our own quiet late bloom, with no other
witness necessary. While wearily I question

the influence of this golden signpost, I
kneel onto the path clothed, but so unadorned

in spirit, run my hands deep through the sand
of this beach I long for real connection with

and remember its scientific name, Solidago,
which in Latin means "to make whole."

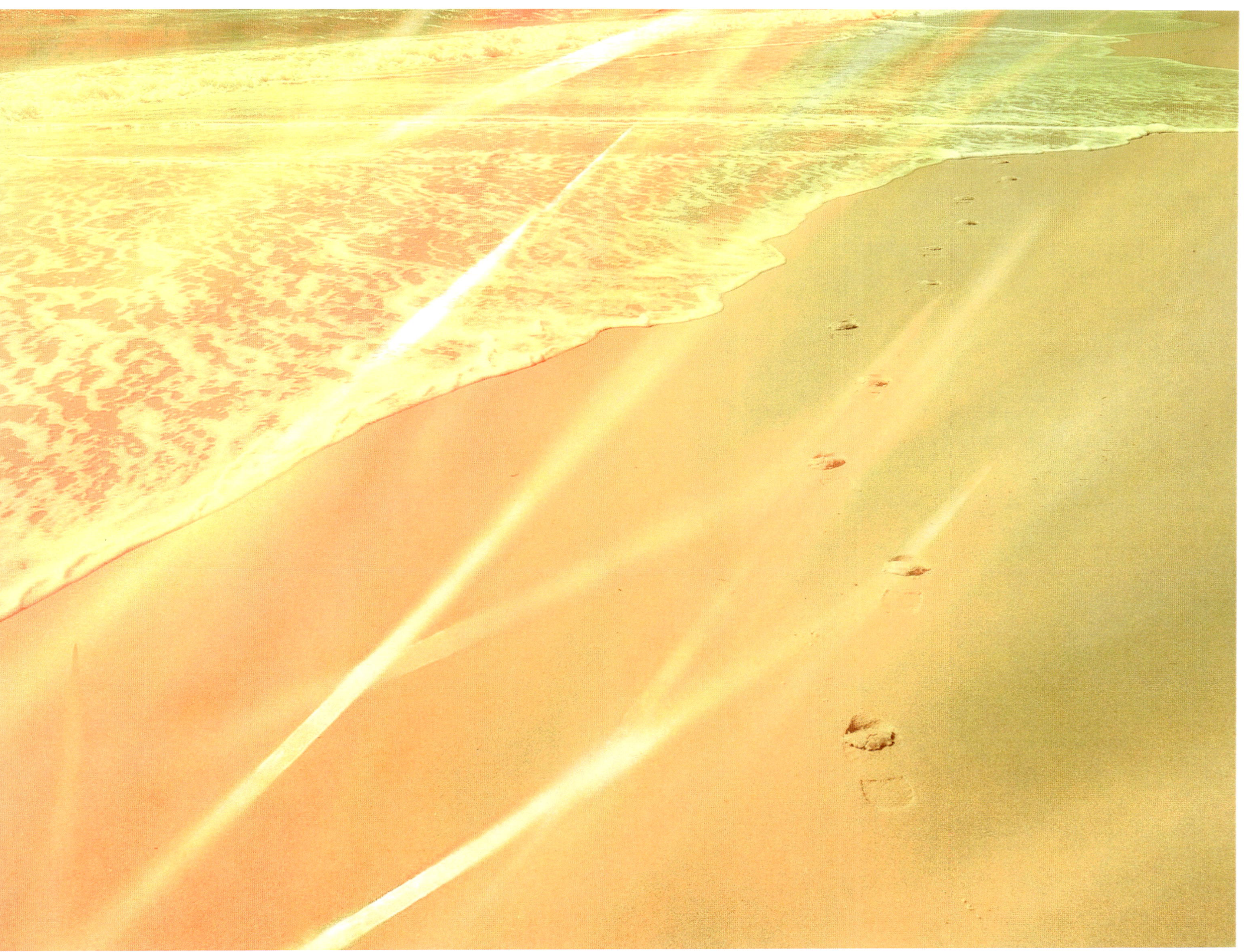

Credo

for my brother

By Brandon Carner
Artwork by Emily Eisen

Absorb the world
Methodically and consistently
Like an efficient arachnid in a high-traffic zone.
Make careful choices about what you let enter your web.

Like a quizzical blue-jay
with its head cocked halfway to the side,
pause to calculate
before you take flight.
Ensure that an unforeseen breeze won't blow you off course.

Life is a roaring samba;
a slow waltz and smooth jazz too.
Be able to shake it to all different flavors of rhythm.

Go through life like a distance runner,
breath carefully paced.
Don't come to die as just another rat who raced.

And when the end of the day comes
and life has entered your soul in such volume
that it leaks from your pores,
make sure to take a moment.

Believe in the blue jay,
who sings its mating call,
and knows that when the right tune is sung back,
It is time to fly away.

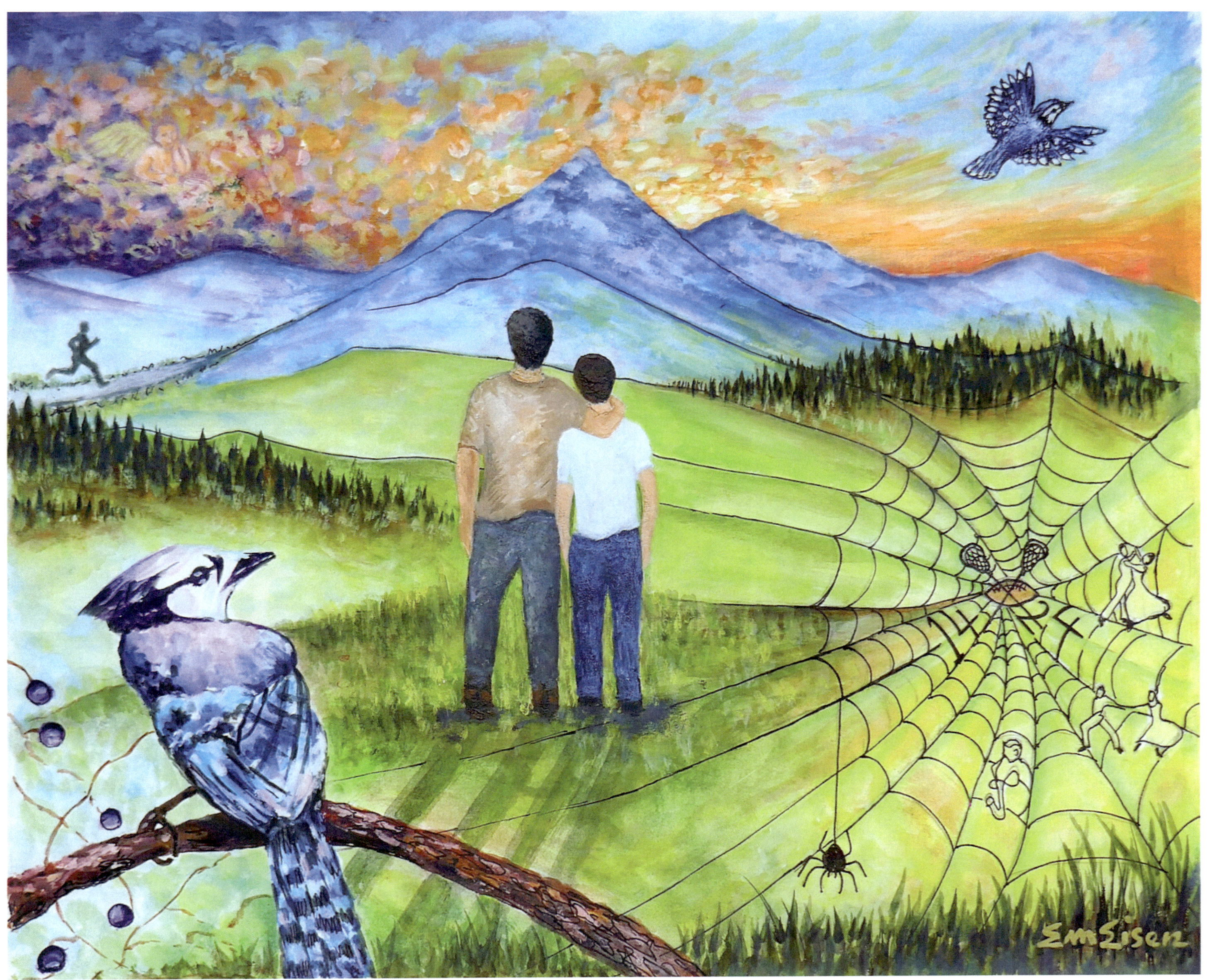

Mother to Mother

Poetry by Vicki Iorio
Artwork by Joe Coen

The geese take over the runway
when production of the F14 shuts down.

Long after their winged visas expire
these immigrants stay

on Long Island, finding the climate
kinder than Canada.

Clipboard in hand, heavy with you,
I waddle into the boneyard in search of scrap metal.

Nesting with her green goslings in a broken cockpit,
a gray mother hisses at me and refuses

to leave the pilot seat even after I flash
my Government ID. I put off the disposal

of this fuselage, while I wait for these fledglings
to become juveniles, for the military

precision of their flyby.

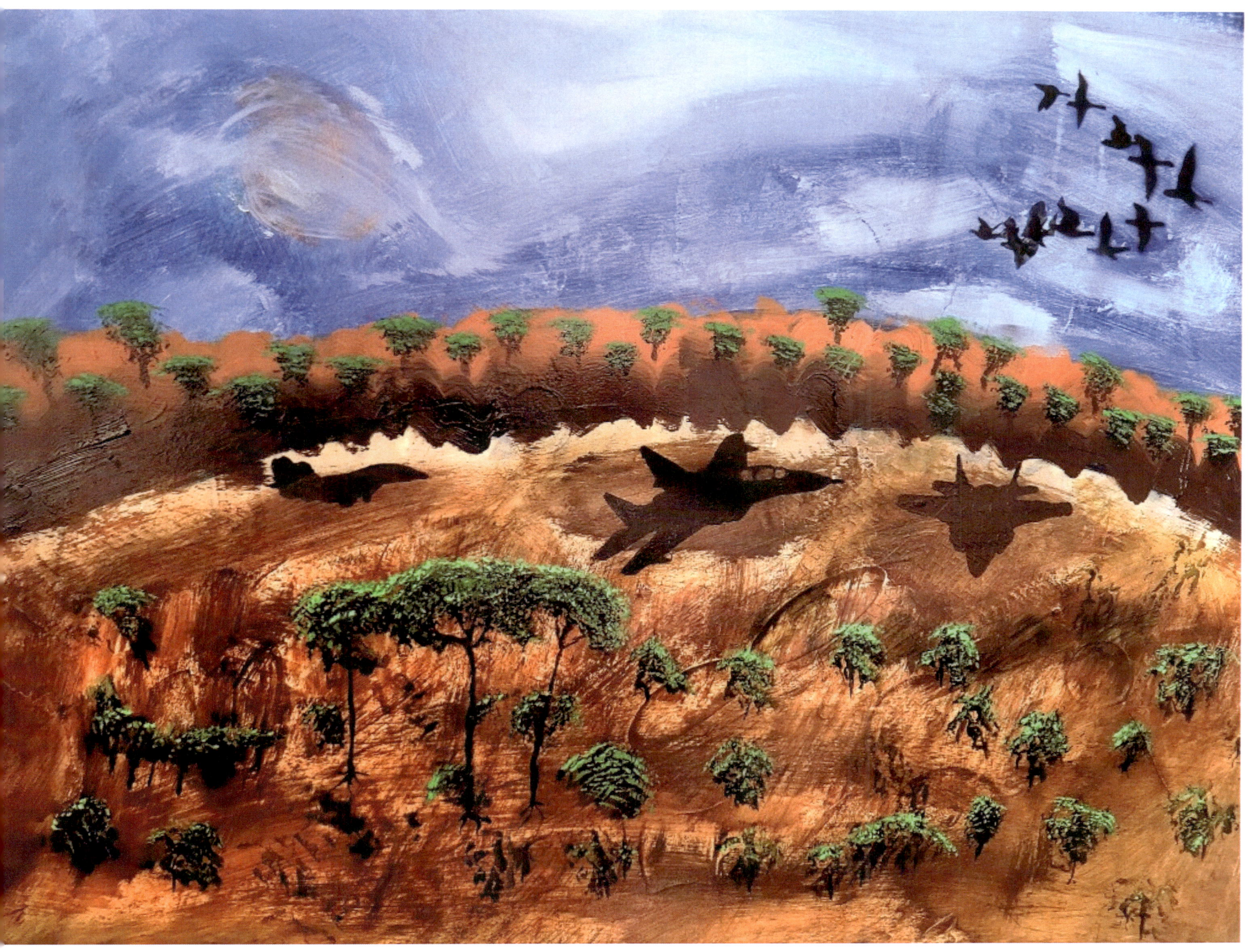

Evergreen

Poetry by Megan Dausch
Artwork by Silvia Maria Rey

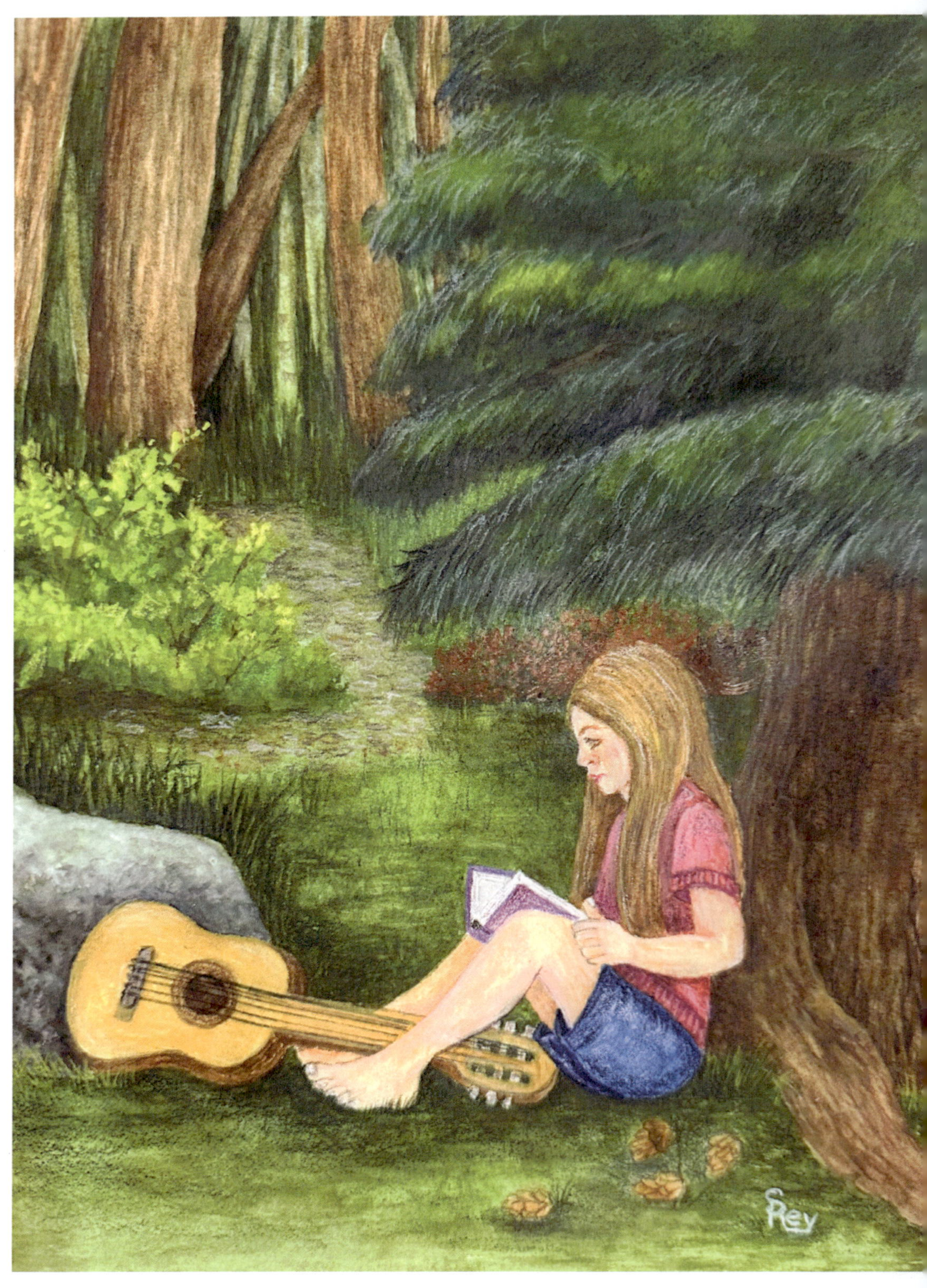

You tower over me.
I trail questions along your scaly bark
yearn to translate your network of vibrant underground language
transmitted through your root tips and fungal friends.

When wind whisks seeds from your cones, and new trees root,
will you nurture your saplings, send them energy until they grow tall enough to meet
light?

When a storm visits
will you become paper, feel fingers murmur over your veneer of braille dots
catch poems tapped out onto your whitewashed surface
transport words that will change lives?

Will you become the hollow body of a guitar
play a song that will unravel a heart
braid it together?
Will you become a piece of a home
shelter lives and generations of dreams?

Or will you continue to thrive right where you stand,
renewing us with oxygen, sustaining life?
Pulling rainwater up through roots,
releasing moisture back into the atmosphere through needles like gentle tears of
gratitude?

We take in each other's exhalations. Use what the other cannot.
I inhale your woody fruity reassurance.
I may never understand your words
but breathing together in your shade is enough.

A Homecoming

By Robert Hodum
Artwork by Vivien Pollack

Seems
Ghost trollies clang down these rails,
Heading hell-bent straight to the harbor this very night.
Their phantoms' brass bells sound high,
Then low like the pitch of the sea,
Past Trinity Church, olde Murphy's, and Skippers too,
Under the glow of a full Wolf Moon.

Buoys clapping hard,
As shore end's pilings groan down deep,
Hold, hold, hold tight!
Mast-slapping halyards
Whipped in January winds,
This port-side cacophony
Sounds a homecoming call,
To invisible, yearning ears.

Winter's shadows whisper ... All clear.
First one, then another, soon more
Shoe-shufflers moving down Main.
The rustle of "old salts" bumming smokes,
Mumbling tales and saucy jokes,
Long lost to one another, seems eons ago,
Blend unhurriedly in a shadowy embrace.

Silhouettes,
Gone missing off shore, in blue water deep,
Taken by wind or storm,
Blown asunder by rock-like sleet.
All summoned by this winter's whistle,
Followed the screak of spirit trolley wheels,
And by the lumen of a January Wolf Moon,
This very night, came home.

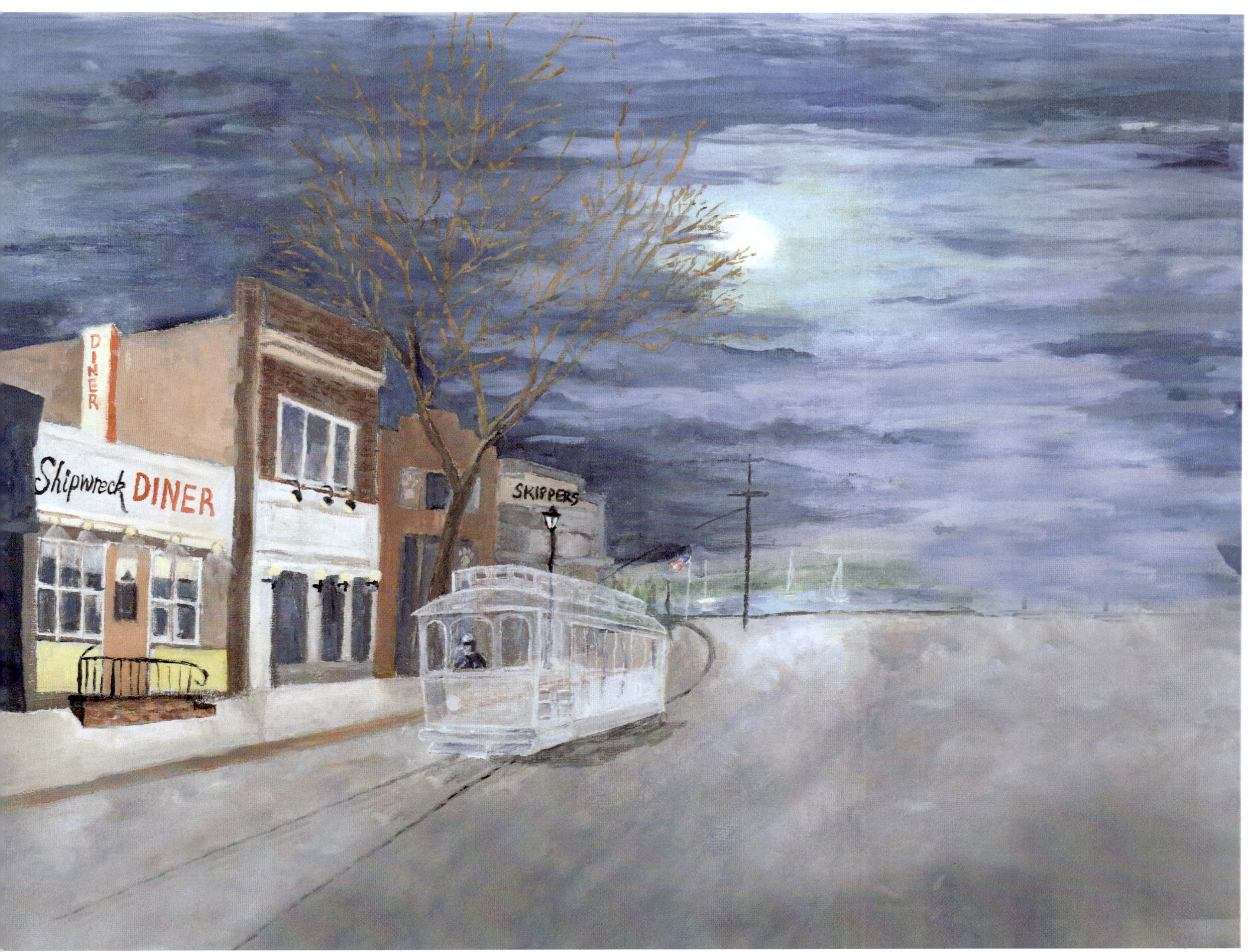
DINER
Shipwreck DINER
SKIPPERS

Provence

Poem by Anne Coen
Artwork by Joan Martorana

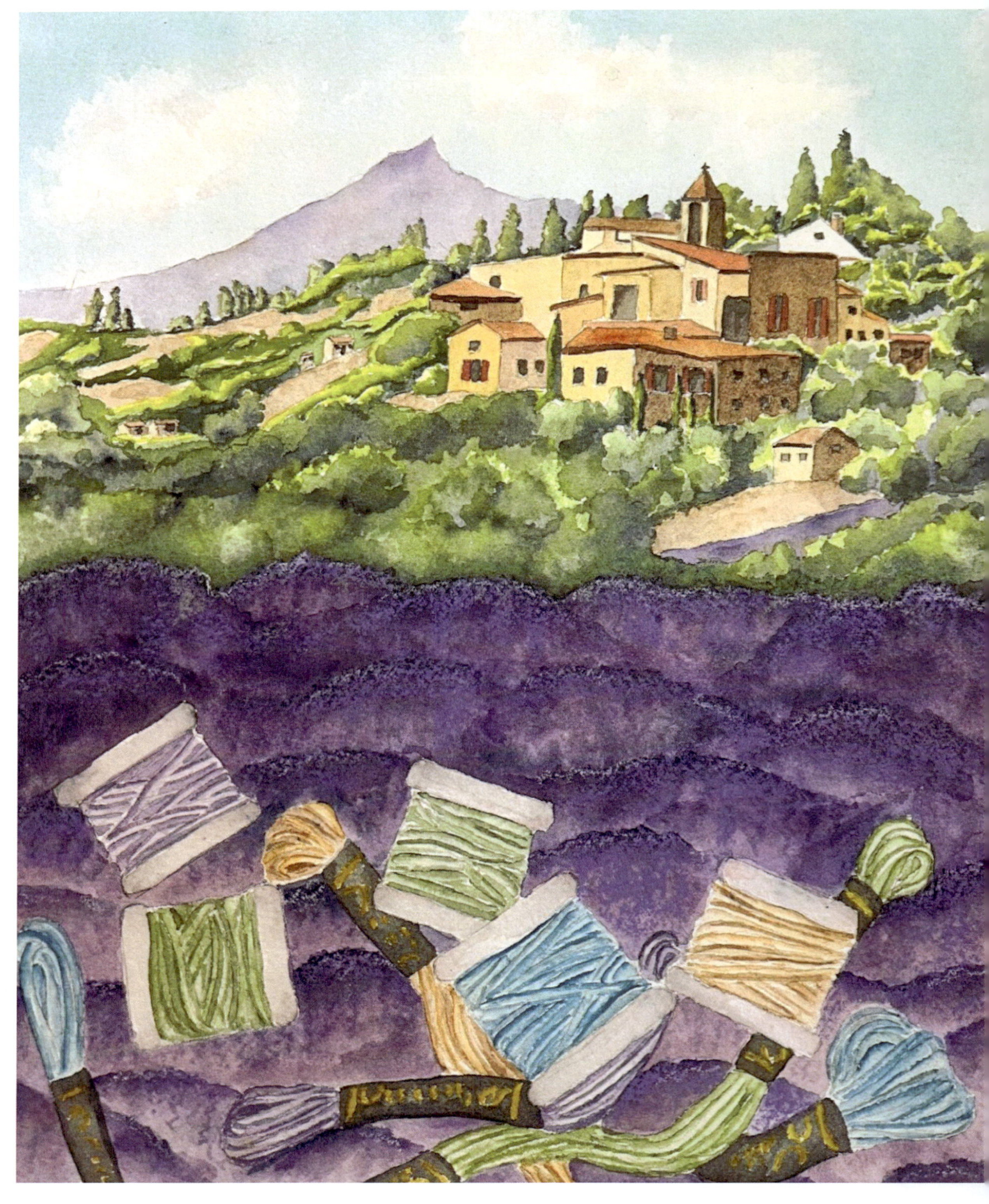

Recovery can be painstakingly slow,
progress measured in miniscule increments,
like work resumed on a counted cross-stitch project
that has been abandoned for months.

It is easy to miscalculate.
Placing stitches incorrectly,
knots and snarls pop up like weeds.
If only the process were as effortless
as unwinding strands of
embroidery floss from paper bobbins.

Completion may be delayed,
but only patience and persistence will transform
an empty field of fabric
into a vibrant pattern of lavender in full bloom
against a cerulean sky.

Cities of Sand and the Sand of Cities

Poetry by Jesse Curran
Artwork by Drigo Morin

Give me such shows–
Give me the streets of Manhattan.
-Walt Whitman

Stripped and shipped from the north shore's silt
two-hundred-million-tons, write the history books,
all that sand to rise Manhattan, to make it new
to make it modern, to make it jazz and clang and shine.
They say the poorly sorted bits of glacial debris
were ideal to mix and forge the scrapers' concrete
and local legend lends that earth cut from the Pit
rolled out the sidewalks that hug the thronged edges
of the avenues. Can you see a young girl digging
and romping in a massive sabulous mound, heaped
on the deck of her grandfather's schooner, a two day
slow sail to midtown to drop the load—how fabulous.
When I walk this beach, my heart ascends like a spire.
When I stroll Fifth Avenue, my soles find the strand
I call home.

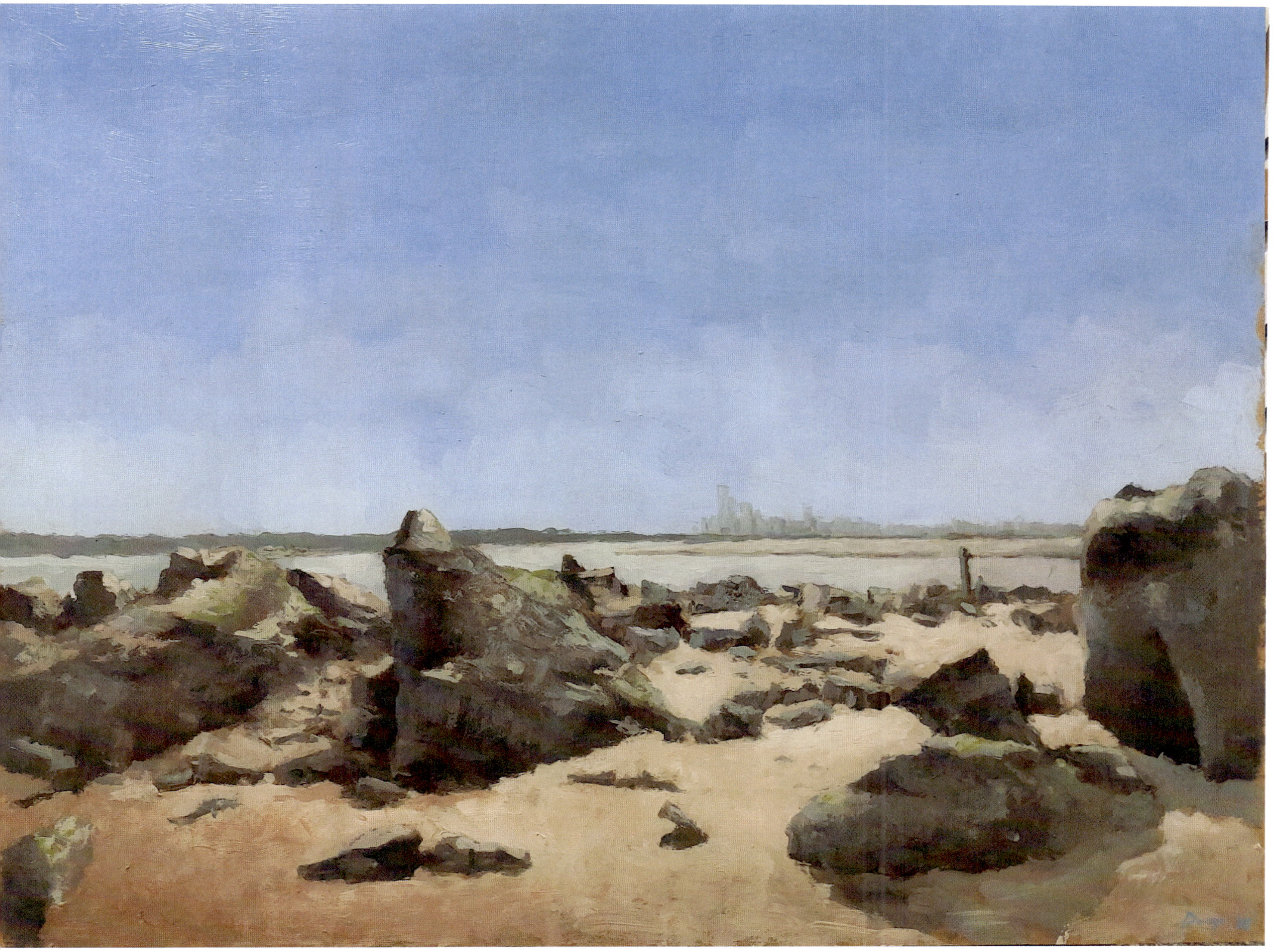

The Marina

Poem by Sarah Goodman
Artwork by David Schram

There's a green grassfield by the docks
Onto which a momentary glance of sunlight hits
And sprays
Like the satiny waves of the water onto concrete rocks

Where time seems to gradually still
And dogs run about and little children twirl
And shout
Like the headstrong winds against flagpost on harsh winter days

Across the bay, sailboats sway on the waves
And musselfinders haul a load to crack open shells
That fell
Which, in turn, are scattered upon the evervast bayshore

Just down the way, shops crop up in an endless row
A variety not unlike its people whom I know

And from atop the hill,
The waters seem an endless depth of satin-top gray-blue well
And on the green grassfield by the bay,
There's a certain charisma which I can't quite name
Watching
Poets spin sugared words like dancers spin to tune
And painters splash their colorstained water on the sills

As time seems to still

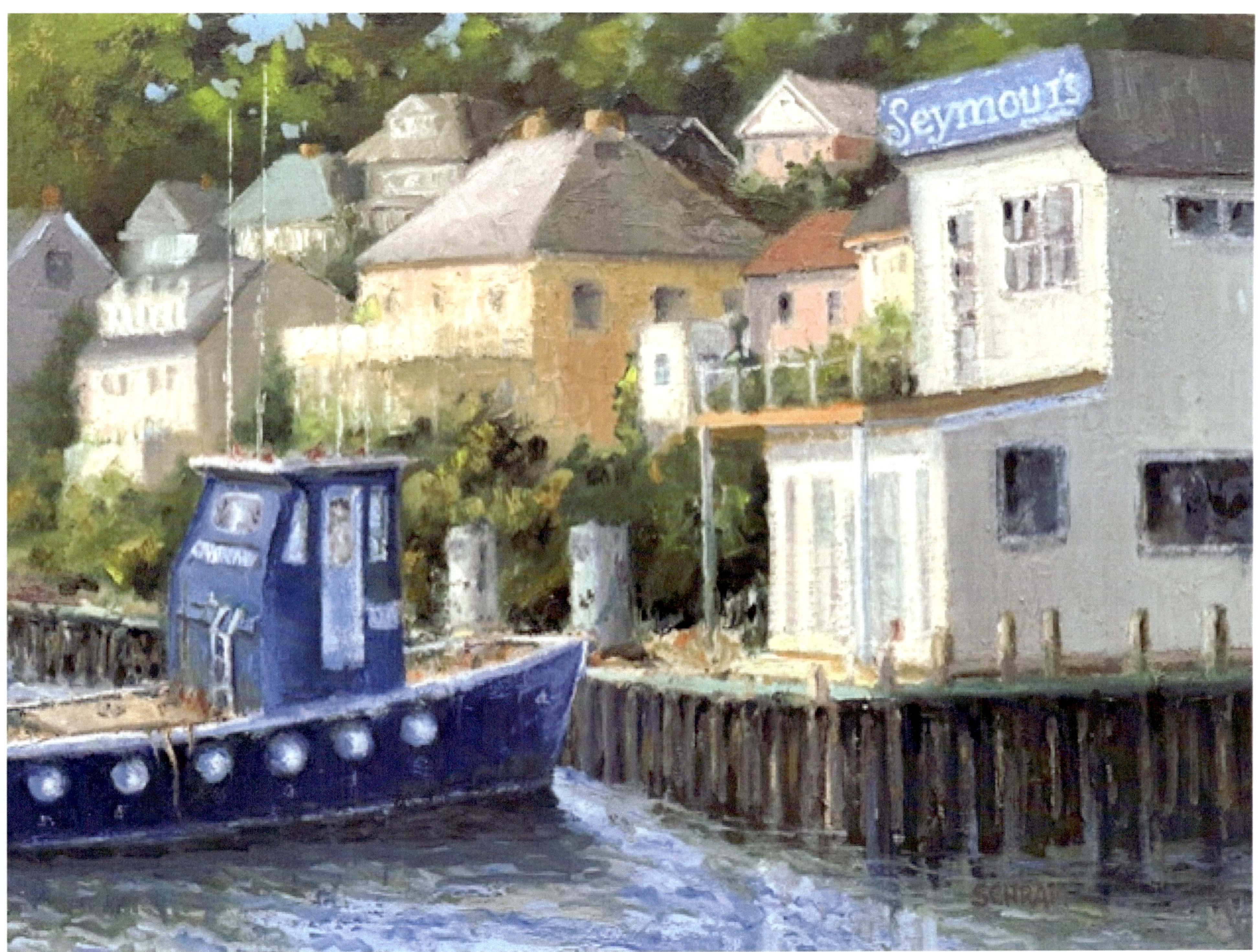
Seymour's

Cow Harbor

by Pamela Kenley-Meschino
Artwork "Lifesaver " by Jan Guarino

has no cows, just people
and dogs, a gathering of boats moored
for summer revelers or wrapped away
from winter winds, an exclamation of buoys
waiting for their return, for winds to direct
their penchant for adventure.

Meanwhile, ducks and cormorants
make a show of indifference, appearing
and disappearing in the rhythmic flow
of the bay, a clamor of geese claims
space across the green.

Cows may have left, but visitors
still arrive to sit and ruminate, drawn
toward the idyllic composition of sea
and sky, the conspiring pink of another
sunset slipping over the hill.

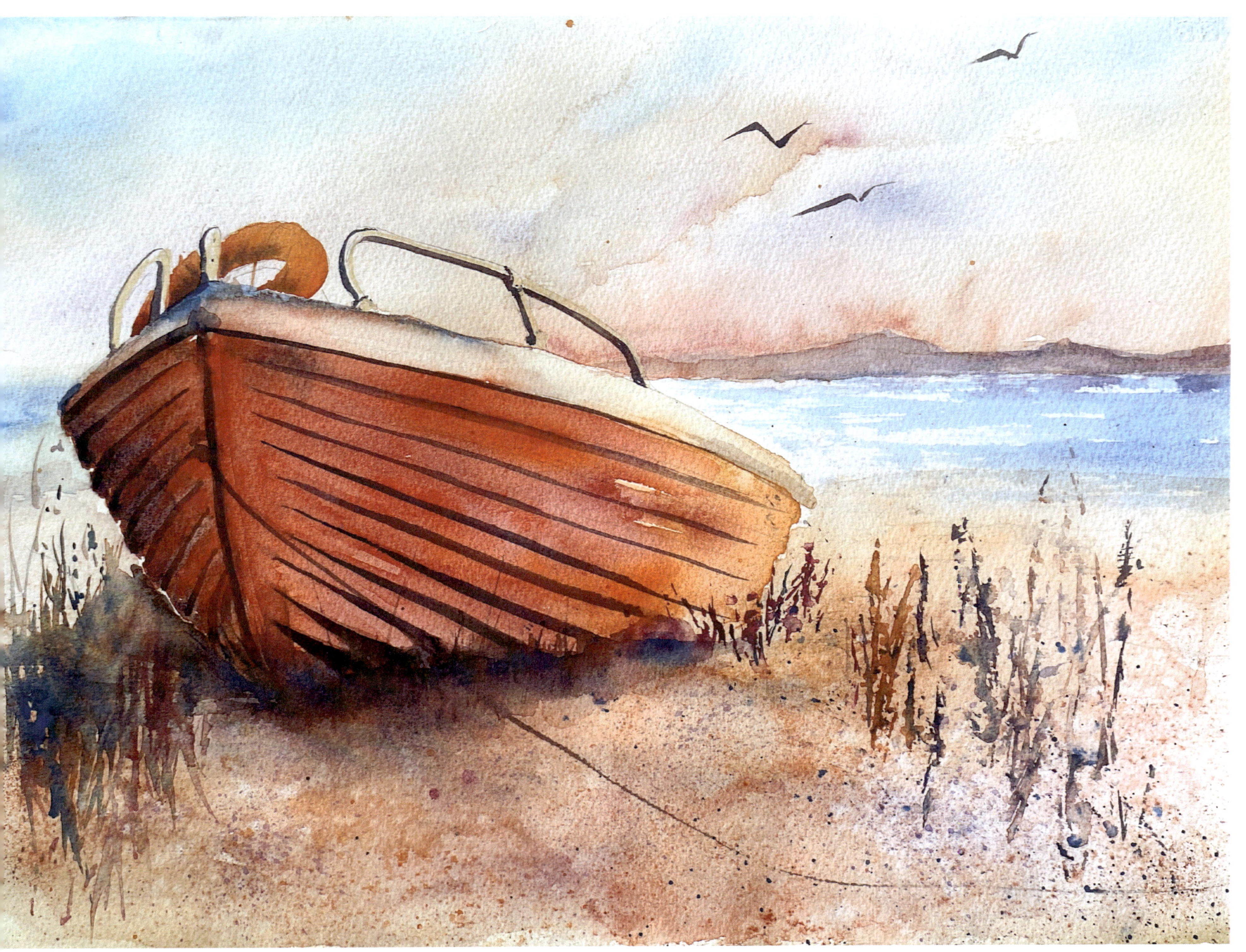

Sea Turtle Maiden

Poem by Margarette Wahl
Artwork by Kathleen Izzo

A want to rescue sea turtles
witness rehabilitation
She hoped to be a sea turtle maiden
Her spirit animal
fins for hands and for feet
with a strong back shell
Like one she envisioned
meditating with a Shaman
swimming between waves
This reason brought her
on the beach New Year's Day
She learned to dispose balloons
they washed up the most
on Long Island beach shores
She cleaned up a sock, a doll leg, paper, bottle caps, a fish hook,
collected with gloves
a claw pole and bucket
Careful combs through seaweed sand rocks
In case any spirited creatures
hid beneath
Over twenty pounds of garbage
collected in two hours
She didn't see her spirit animal
only felt their presence close
with each claw grab
Not the sea turtle maiden journey
she had envisioned
Still she was their difference

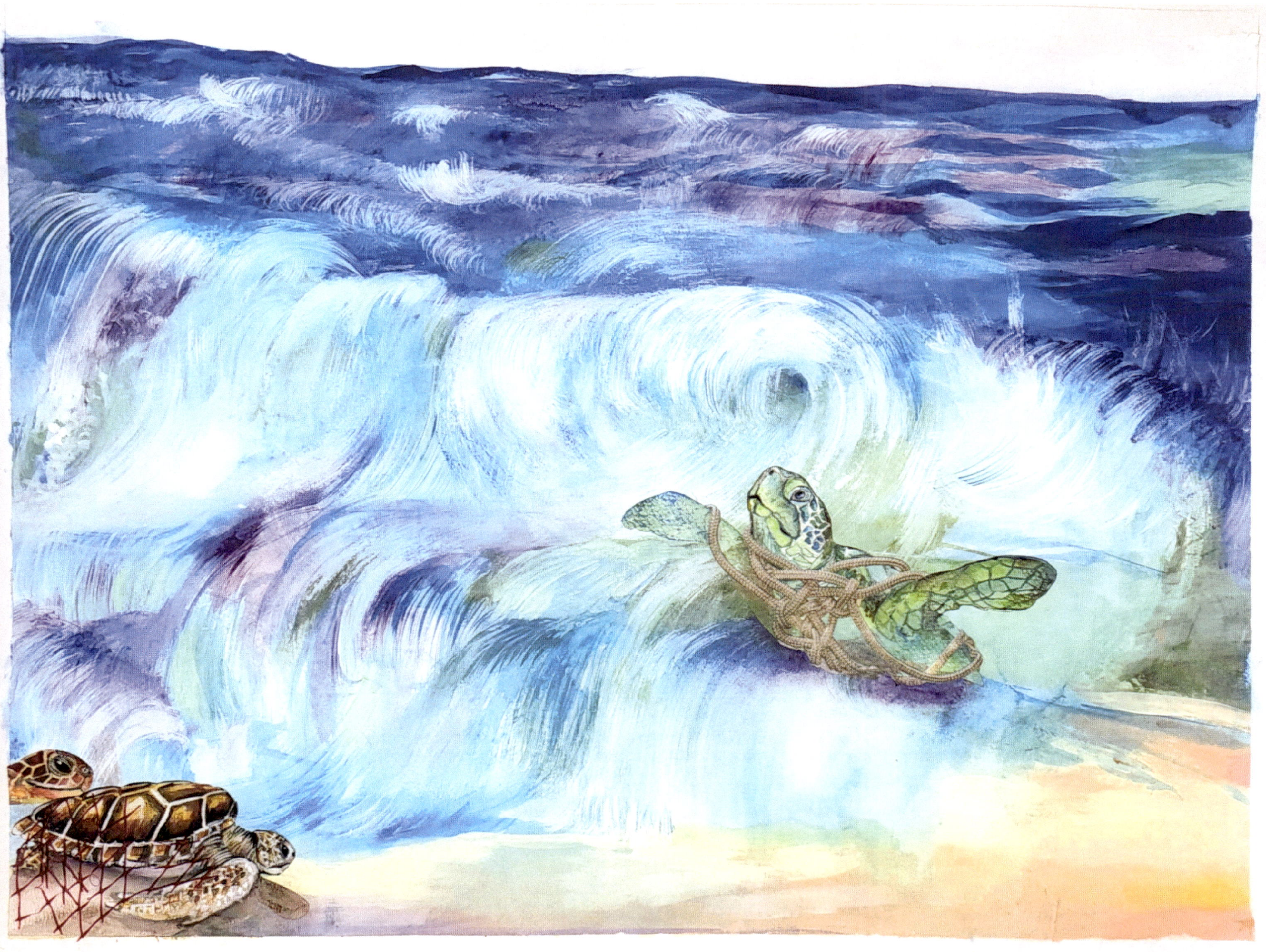

A Royal Wedding

Poem by Kathleen Izzo

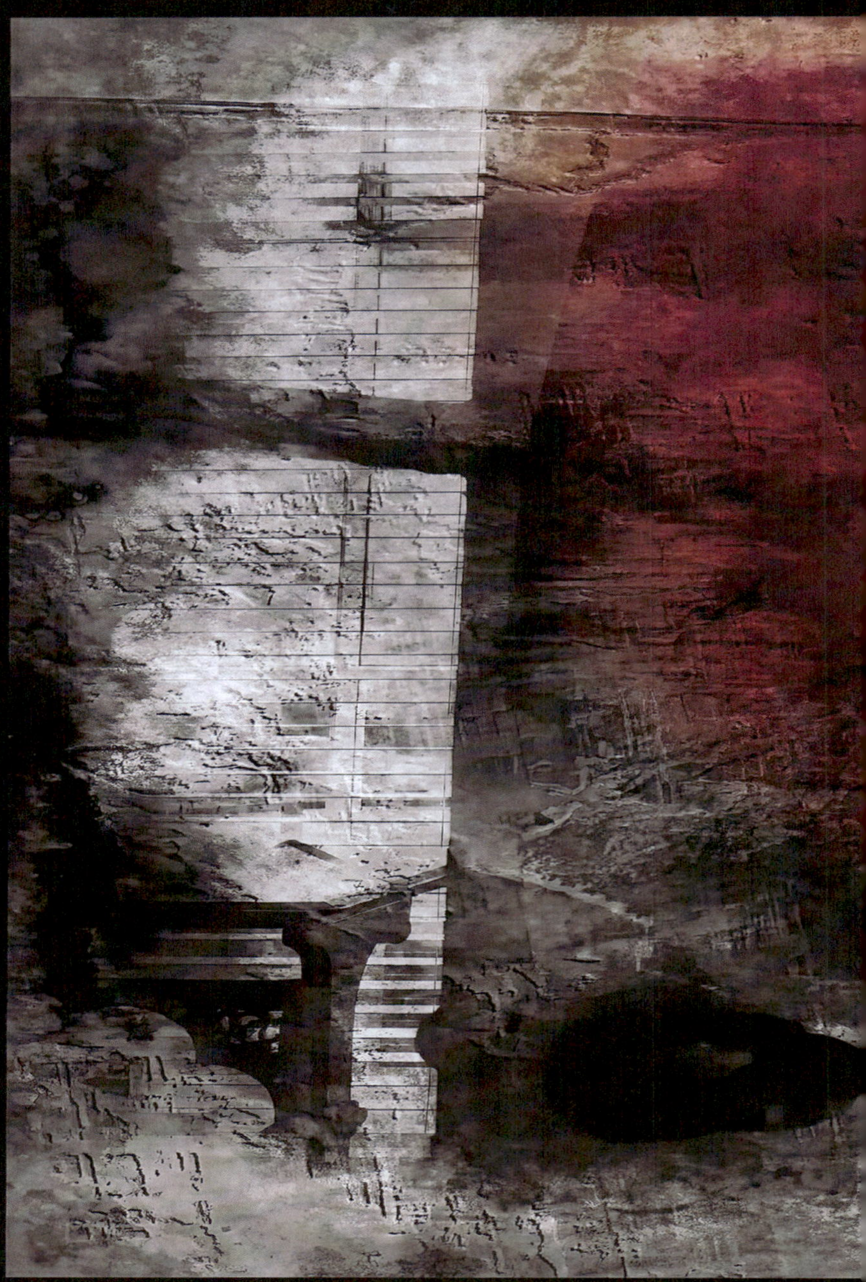

In Radiant Glory, He calls out to me,
Come hither My fair one and sit at My feet.

My love, I Am awaiting thee to ravish your very soul,
My Spirit is penetrating, to purify and make you whole.

My garments they are spotless, My locks are dripping with myrrh,
I entreat you child to open your heart, that I must awaken, stir.

My eyes are brightly shining, My hands with love I caress,
I desire our lives to be entwined, as on
e knitted together and blessed.

My eyes endued with kindness, My tongue a double-edged sword,
Your heart fully laced with precious jewels, shall be your great reward.

My dove and dearest fair one, the apple of My eye,
I'm sick with love for you My prize, I espouse you to be My bride.

I've planned an awesome wedding day with garments white as snow,
Crowns of gold shall adorn your face, so I can see your radiant glow.

You'll meet Me at the altar there, with your hand reached out to Mine,
I'll long to see your love-sick eyes, when I remove your veil, you'll shine.

And hand in hand we'll take our vows, declaring a lifetime covenant,
No man shall separate our bond, nor remove the joy we've spent.

And as we marvel in our love, with doves fluttering near, above,
Your kisses shall entreat My face, like hands fitting in a glove.

My purpose for us is to become, a couple finely woven,
Together we'll win the souls of men, whose lives I've handpicked chosen.

Then I'll entreat you to come to Me, to find your place on earth,
I'm standing here awaiting your love, for I've known you before your birth.

When Dogma Turned to Dust

Artwork by Jennifer A. Uihlein

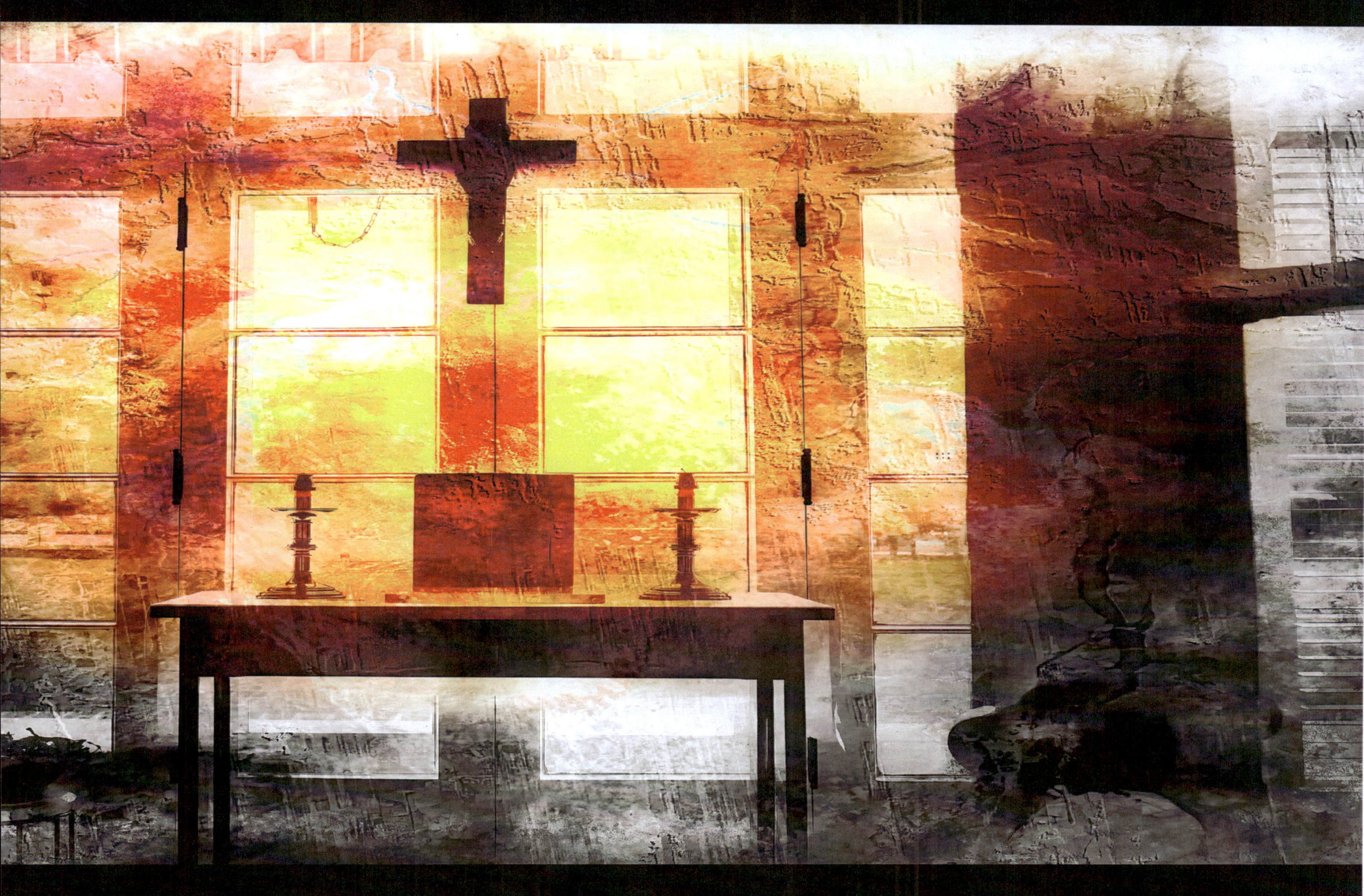

The Blue Jay

by Darren Sardelli
Artwork by Tiffany Asadourian

As I sit,
and think,
and write,
I see a blue jay—
blue and white.
Quiet.
Graceful.
Fearless.
Free.
A work of art.
A joy to see.
I wonder how
it came to be.

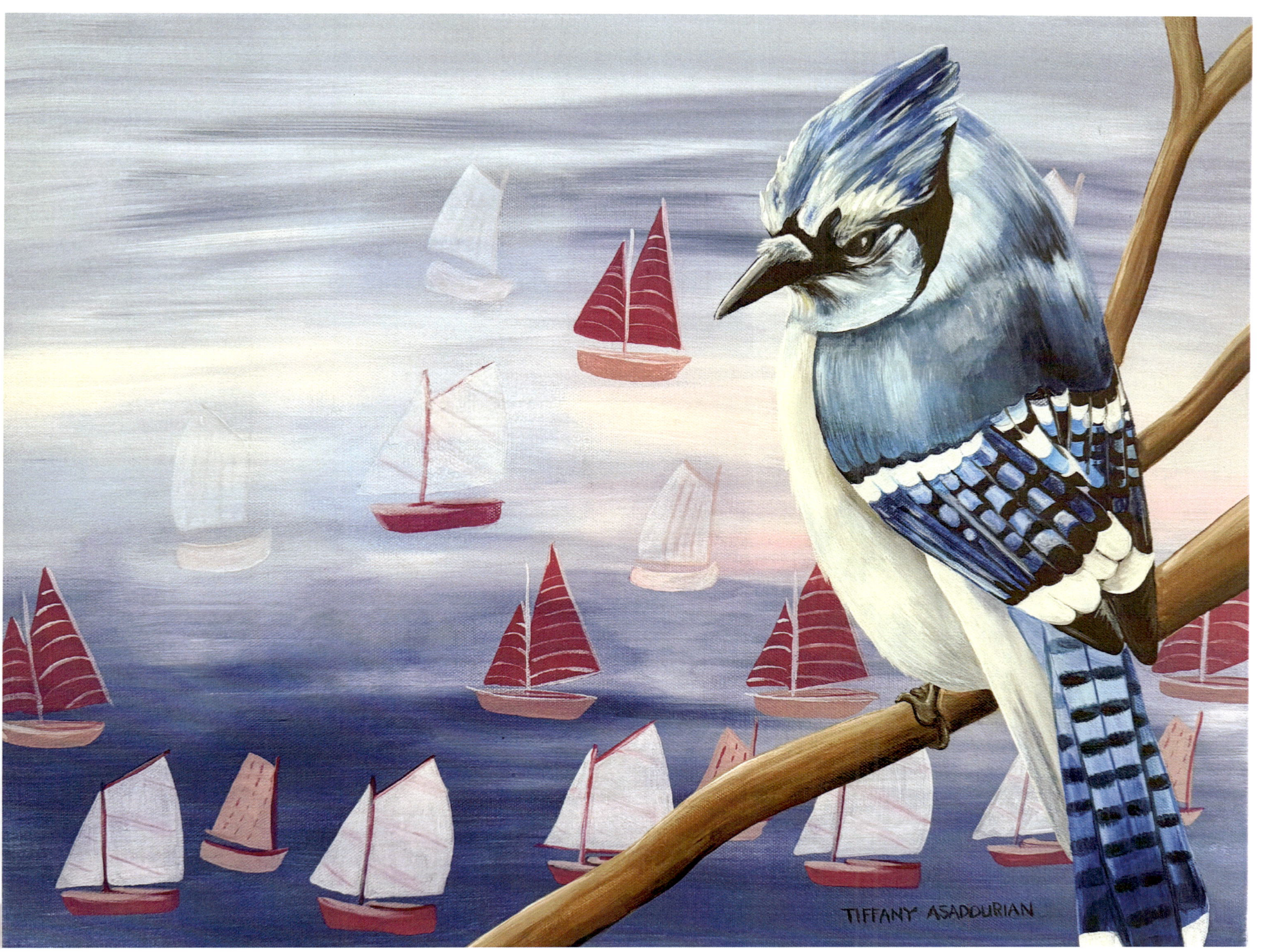
TIFFANY ASADOURIAN

ARTIST AND POET BIOS

Tiffany Asadourian is an artist originally from Northern California, now rooted in the serene beauty of Northport with her husband, where they raise their three sons. Her father, an artist himself, ignited her passion for creating works that honor life's vibrancy and the world around her. Her art-spanning paintings, mosaics, and photography draw from nature, with a focus on birds and landscapes, while also weaving in personal experiences and emotions. The profound loss of her father has taught her to embrace each moment, infusing her work with themes of love, hope, and resilience.

Richard Bronson is on the faculty of the Center for Medical Humanities, Compassionate Care & Bioethics of the Renaissance School of Medicine at Stony Brook University. He is a member of the boards of the Walt Whitman Birthplace and the Long Island Poetry Collective, is the recipient of the Leonard Tow Humanism in Medicine Award of the Arnold P. Gold Foundation, and served as Poet Laureate of Suffolk County 2021 – 2023.

Brandon Carner lived in his cherished hometown of Northport for twenty-one years. With a smile and true affection, Brandon was devoted to family, friends, sports, conversation and the written word. He enjoyed poetry at a deep level and relished the ability to work with language in new ways. "Credo" was written while he attended Washington and Lee University. Brandon's love for his brother shines through this poem.

Lisa Carrano has been an artist her whole life. Different times, happenings and experiences inspire her to create. The poem "Veterans" inspired her to show her patriotism for our country. Lisa's artwork depicts a soldier saluting, but really the artwork is her salute to them. Not coming from a military background, she only has the utmost admiration and respect for those willing to serve, for the rest of us. She still gets emotional when she sees service men and women in uniform.

Loretta Cerame is a professional artist living in East Northport, NY. Originally from Brooklyn, Loretta received her BFA in Graphic Arts from New York Institute of Technology in 1990. After a long hiatus from art, she has ignited her inner artist and embarked on a journey of creative exploration - painting with acrylics, oils, mixed media and gouache. Loretta works intuitively letting her brush lead the way! Her art is a reawakening and deeper exploration of the heART; connecting to the creator within. All she creates is encoded with the energies of Love, Peace and Unity. May her work evoke and awaken thy Love within. Instagram @letyourheartshinebrightly

Anne Coen is a retired special education teacher who ventured into performance poetry when she accidentally signed a clipboard during an open mic. She has featured for local libraries, the Oceanside Gazebo, and Pagan-Fletcher Restoration. Her work has been published in many Long Island Anthologies.

Joe Coen is an abstract artist and the other half of a poetic duo with his wife Anne. He is co-host of Poetry at the Pagan summer series, and has featured at Sip This, Bellmore Memorial Library, and Poets in Port. His work has been published in Poets4Paris, Balance 2016, PPA Literary Review, and Bards Annual. He was First Runner Up in the LI Light Poetry Competition.

Jesse Curran is a poet, essayist, scholar, and teacher who lives in Northport, NY. Her essays and poems have appeared in dozens of literary journals, including Literary Mama, Radical Teacher, Oyster River Pages, Blueline, and Ruminate. She is the 2025 Long Island Poet of the Year and teaches in the Department of English at SUNY Old Westbury. www.jesseleecurran.com

Megan Dausch has been creating stories and poems since childhood. Megan lives on Long Island, where she makes her home with her husband and guide dog. Her recent work has appeared in Breath and Shadow, Star 82 Review, Fresh Words, Claw & Blossom, and Bards Annual. Drawing from her experiences as a blind woman, her writing explores life through imagery and sensory language. When Megan isn't writing, she works as an Accessibility Specialist.

Emily Eisen lives in Northport, NY. She is a fine artist, illustrator, singer-songwriter, and mentor. She exhibits her art at The Northport Firefly Artists Gallery as well as locally and nationally. Her inspiration rises from her love of the land and sea, the colors and rhythms of nature, and the heart and soul of the human spirit. She loves to sing, dance, swim, hike, read, compose music, teach yoga, enjoy the arts and time with her friends, family, and grandchildren.

Deidre Elzer-Lento, President of Huntington Camera Club, is an accomplished photographer who enjoys photographing, manipulating, and sharing her images. She teaches photography, lectures, and judges photographic exhibitions. Deidre's work resides in the permanent collections of museums and businesses. She's been published in books, newspapers, and magazines. Her photos have graced the covers of magazines, received top awards in photo contests, and aired on television. She displays her work in Firefly Artists' Gallery and calls the North Shore her home.

Sarah Goodman is the 2024-2026 Suffolk County Teen Poet Laureate. Sarah has organized and run programming for teens and children at libraries and schools across Suffolk County. She has been published in several anthologies and magazines, and has hosted and featured at various poetry open mics. She has also organized and judged the first Suffolk Youth Poetry Competition. Sarah has had a long-standing passion for philanthropy for at-risk youth and pancreatic cancer foundations.

Jan Guarino is a graduate of the Fashion Institute of Technology and has recently retired from graphic design to focus entirely on her painting and teaching careers. She guides students to enjoy the beauty and fun of this medium. Those very skills she learned in college are ones she accesses to this day when painting and teaching watercolors. Jan offers in-person watercolor workshops at the Landgrove Inn in Vermont, The Omega Institute, on location in Italy, and the Palm Beach Watercolor Society, as well as weekly at the Huntington Arts Council on Long Island. Her work can be seen in Creations Magazine on the Poetry Page and occasionally on the cover. She is a member of the Firefly Artists Gallery and is also at The Nest on Main Street in Northport. On National Authors Day - November 1st - she self-published her first book, "Thinking Your Way Through Watercolors," which can be found on Amazon.

Robert Hodum, known as "Pop Pop" to his grandchildren, enjoys sharing his writings with them. Catching Winds North, his poetry, celebrates the beauty of Long Island and the joys and challenges of daily life. Conversations On La Playa recounts his adventures in Colombia, South America. Pilgrims' Steps is a history of pilgrimage to Santiago de Compostela and its namesake, Saint James the Greater. Just Messing Around recounts the author's exploits in the potato fields and woods of East Northport, Long Island in the early 1960s. Bone Dust, tales of horror, magical realism, and the supernatural world, are not shared with the kiddos.

Vicki Iorio can't sing or do backflips, so she writes. Iorio is the author of the poetry collections Poems from the Dirty Couch (Local Gems Press), Not Sorry (Alien Buddha Press), and the chapbooks Send Me a Letter (dancinggirlpress), Something Fishy (Finishing Line Press), and The Blabbermouth (Alien Buddha Press). Iorio's poetry has appeared in numerous print and on-line journals. When she's not writing, you can find her sweating on her Peloton or drinking a nice crisp white wine.

Kathleen Izzo is a mixed-media artist, poet, and teacher who has been developing her art since she was a small child. In her earliest years, Kathleen exhibited interest in putting things together to make artistic sculptures from found objects. Her art is autobiographical in nature, depicting her deep Christian faith and her relationship with a loving God. Most of her images emanate directly from the Lord God through her daily prayer and worship. Website: KATHIZO.COM

Pamela Kenley-Meschino is originally from the UK, where she developed a love of nature, poetry, and music, thanks in part to the influence of her Irish mother. Her poetry has appeared in Literal Latté, Bards Annual anthologies, The New Verse News, The Stafford Challenge Anthology, and has been featured on WNYC's 2025 poetry month presentations. She is an educator whose classes explore the connection between writing and healing as well as the importance of shared stories.

Brian Leahy's work can be seen on the bookmark for The View From Here, the 2025 Poetry Path Publication. Brian is an illustration student at SVA trying to express themselves creatively with mostly pen and ink work. They like to break out and try different techniques or colors, but pen and ink is what mostly calls to them!

Joan Vera Martorana began exploring art at an early age. From paper art to recycled sculptures, it was when Joan experienced working in oils that her love of painting evolved. After retiring from teaching, Joan devoted her time to watercolors, developing her skills of capturing the beauty of nature around her, focusing on florals and scenery. Joan captures the clarity and brightness of her subjects. Joan Vera's paintings can be seen at various art shows throughout Suffolk County. Her work has national as well as international acclaim.

Drigo Morin received his BFA in Illustration from the School of Visual Arts in New York City. He has also studied at The Art Students League NYC and The Stevenson Academy on Long Island. An oil painter of still life and portraits, he has been concentrating on landscapes the last few years.

Nancy Panicucci-Roma is a photography enthusiast who has a deep passion for nature, wildlife and humanitarian causes. She lives in Northport but her roots are in Rockland County where she had a 36 year long career in mental health. Nancy is dedicated to her photography, connecting with people of like mind, capturing images of natural beauty and sharing her passion with others. Some of her images can be seen on her instagram page @nancyphotoroma.

Vivien Pollack began her art career as a Textile Designer, designing for the textile print industry in NYC and creating original designs that were sold to manufacturers. She has since exhibited many award winning paintings in galleries and shows. Besides painting on silk, she works with oils and pastels.

Diana Poulos-Lutz has an M.A. in Political Science from Long Island University, as well as an M.Phil. in Politics from The New School for Social Research. Diana's poems have won numerous local awards and an international award. Diana has published two poetry books, Time to Rise and I Walk On. Her poetry is inspired by her love of nature, mindfulness, equality, and empowerment.

JoAnn Proscia loves Northport. She's lived here for fifty-three years. She and her late husband John raised their two sons, David and Douglas, here. She also loves writing. Her poetry has been published in anthologies and magazines. A friend who lives in Brunei turned one of her poems into a song he wrote. She has an MFA in Creative Writing and Literature from Southampton Stony Brook. She has led writing groups and currently leads film discussions at the Northport Library.

Silvia María Rey is an educator, author, and award-winning artist. Originally from Havana, Cuba, she immigrated to the United States in 1961. She received a Bachelor of Fine Arts degree from Herbert H. Lehman College. She went on to receive several advanced certificates and degrees in the field of education focusing on the literacy needs of bilingual students and second language learners. She published her first book in November 2020 *In the Eyes of the Beholder*. Her most recent book *Through my Mother's Words*, a memoir based on her mother's poetry documenting her life in Cuba and the United States was published in 2024. Silvia is an Associate Member of The Pastel Society of America (PSA), a Signature Member of the National Association of Women Artists (NAWA) She is a resident artist at The Firefly Artists Gallery where she exhibits her work. She lives on Long Island with her son, daughter-in-law and a menagerie of fur, finned and feathered babies.

Darren Sardelli's poems are featured in 31 children's books in the U.S. and U.K. His poetry is also being showcased in middle schools, high schools, and universities all over the world. He's done over 1,000 school visits, plays ice hockey, and enjoys traveling with his beautiful wife and two amazing sons. You can learn more about Darren at www.LaughAlotPoetry.com

David Schram is a member of the Huntington Arts Council, and lives in Northport, NY with his family. He writes:
On a fateful day in 2007, while walking my dog Simon in Northport park, I met the amazing artist Ward Hooper. He was working on a colorful and loose plein air painting of the harbor. Within weeks I started to take his watercolor classes at the Art League of Long Island and was soon hooked on painting. Ward is now 96 yrs young and still painting. We have remained good friends ever since. My new love for painting strongly influenced my decision to leave behind a 35 year corporate level business career to leisurely pursue a more (frustrating) creative path and focus. After retiring, I began to take weekly workshops with the very talented (and always humorous) artist Howard Rose and slowly transitioned from watercolor to mostly painting with oils. My subjects range from Northport village landscapes and seascapes to people in motion. I am attracted to the light, shadows and interplay of color and always looking to capture the aesthetically pleasing aspects of the place or the uniqueness of the subject. Never realistic, not totally impressionistic, somewhere in between? My creative process often resembles a mad dash ... with frequent sidetracks into the land of procrastination. When inspiration strikes, I try to get lots of paint down on canvas quickly, working fast to get the composition and values correct, then usually go back to get the composition correct! My passion for painting has given me an alternative sense of purpose and a creative outlet. I regularly exhibit my work in local shows around Long Island and am honored to have one of my paintings chosen to be displayed on the Northport Poetry Path.

Emily-Sue Sloane is an award-winning poet who writes about the wonder and the worry of the human connection. Her work has been published in numerous journals, anthologies and on Northport's inaugural Poetry Path. She is the author of two poetry books, We Are Beach Glass (2022) and Disconnects and Other Broken Threads (The Poetry Box, March 2024). She lives in Huntington Station, NY, with her wife, singer-songwriter Linda Sussman. For more, please visit https://EmilySueSloane.com.

Jennifer A. Uihlein is an award-winning photographer, independent documentary filmmaker, gallery curator, and live sports broadcast operator. She believes that stories, whether seen or spoken, can connect, disrupt, and heal. Through Girl in a Camera Productions (girlinacamera.com), she captures moments through event photography, photojournalism, and live sports. Her fine art finds voice through Jennifer A. Uihlein Design Studio (jenniferuihlein.com). Her vodcast, Unscripted: Artists Outside the Frame (artistsoutsidetheframe.com), launching fall 2025, amplifies Long Island's diverse art community through inclusive storytelling.

Margarette Wahl is a poet from Massapequa, NY. She has four chapbooks with Local Gems Press and a self-published poetry memoir to her late crush. Margarette is an advisor on the NCPLS, cohost for PPA, and a member of Bards Initiative. Her poem was inspired by beach cleanups, she attended with the organization AMSEAS.